Dinner b

TITLE I

Written by Claire Daniel
Illustrated by Marilyn Mets

"I want to eat," said Mike.

"I do, too," said Kim.

"Mom comes home at five," said Kim. "And she may be tired. Let's cook dinner!"

"What will we make?" said Mike.

"Mom likes pizza," said Kim. "She likes salad. Let's make pizza and salad!"

"Great!" said Mike. "But can we fix all that by five?"

"Sure!" said Kim. "Watch me now!"

"A little bit of this."

"A little bit of that."

"Mix it up."

"Fix it up."

"How about that?"

"I liked that," said Mike. "Now you watch me."

"A little bit of this."

"A little bit of that."

"Mix it up."

"Fix it up."

"How about that?"

9

"Dad, we did it!" said Mike.

"Now we have to cook the pizza," said Kim.

"Good," said Dad.

"I'll help you do that."

"Mom will like this nice dinner," said Dad. "But she won't like the mess. So we have to fix it."

"Wipe a bit of this."

"Wipe a bit of that."

"Mix it up."

"Fix it up."

"How about that?"

13

Mom came in and smiled.

"Hi, kids!" she said. "Oh, how nice! Pizza and salad for dinner."

Mike and Kim and Dad smiled, too.

"And we made the dinner!" said Mike.

"I love this dinner," said Mom. "And best of all — there's no mess!"